DISCOVERING
GOD'S
GOODNESS

women of faith™

DISCOVERING GOD'S GOODNESS

BY

CHRISTA KINDE

FOREWORD BY

LUCI SWINDOLL

THOMAS NELSON
Since 1798

ISBN 978-0-310-68257-8

First Printing May 2016 / Printed in the United States of America

↗ CONTENTS ↖

CONTENTS

⫸ FOREWORD ⫷

My mother was a great cook. I'll never forget her best meal—made with much love and care—fried chicken, macaroni and cheese, hot rolls, lettuce and tomato salad, and corn on the cob. Every bite was delicious, and the minute grace was uttered, my dad and us three hungry kids plowed into that food like hired hands.

Oh, I almost forgot—she would also make Osgood pie. Ever heard of Osgood pie? Oh my! It's fabulous—made with sugar, raisins, chopped pecans, cinnamon, eggs, etc.—all mixed together, baked, and served with ice cream. At this very moment, I'm reading the recipe in Mother's tattered old cookbook from the 1940s, and if I listen carefully, I can still hear her voice as she's serving up the pieces: "Now, for goodness' sake, don't eat the whole thing!"

I used to wonder what "for goodness' sake" meant, but after all these years I think I've figured it out. It means, "that which is to our advantage or enhancement." In other words, Mother knew our inclination to eat too much dessert in one sitting, so she was warning us against a sugar overload. She was saying that it was to our advantage to eat some things in small amounts! But when we think of receiving the goodness of God, it's just the opposite. He serves up truth, mercy, grace, peace, and freedom in abundance. And He invites us to enjoy all of it in abundance! As the psalmist says in Psalms 25:7: "according to Your mercy remember me, for Your goodness sake, O LORD" (NKJV).

This study guide is designed to help all of us enjoy the banquet God gives us every minute of the day according to His goodness. There are chapters, questions, suggestions, definitions, verses, and quizzes, beautifully written and offered to help you understand what's available to you as you become more and more intimately acquainted with the Lord through His Word. I encourage you to sit down at His table of love and dish up a full plate of spiritual food. It will feed your soul and equip you to receive God's incredible goodness. His bounty overflows, so you are about to experience a wonderful feast. And for goodness' sake, you don't ever have to stop eating!

Surely your goodness and unfailing love
will pursue me all the days of my life,
and I will live in the house of the Lord forever.

Psalm 23:6 NLT

—*Luci Swindoll*

❧ INTRODUCTION ❧

Imagine this. You're in a dungeon. Your cell is dark and dank. The floor is scattered with musty straw. Chains anchor you to the wall. There is no window—no glimpse of sky, no breath of fresh air. The only sounds you hear are the drip of condensation off bare stone and the rustle of rats. You crouch in the corner—listless, hopeless, defeated. Then you hear something unexpected. The crash of a distant door, the clamor of running feet. A key scrapes in the door to your cell, and the door swings open. There stands a rescuer, a knight in shining armor. He bends down and removes your chains and lifts you to your feet. "Come, let's get you out of here." But you pull away and back against the wall. "There must be some mistake. You must be looking for some other prisoner." With a tilt of the head, He asks, "And why do you think that?" Shrugging, you reply, "Well, because I committed a crime. I'm guilty. I deserve to be here. You should be looking for someone who is innocent and doesn't belong here at all." With a nod of understanding, He takes your hand, "I know all that, but it's you I've come for. Don't you want to be free? I have come to set you free."

Unexpected mercy. God, in His goodness, sent Jesus to set the captives free. We were guilty, deserving of death, and living without hope when the door swung open. Unmerited favor. Jesus made it possible for our crimes to be forgiven, for our guilty verdict to be overturned, for our record to be wiped clean. Grace. The happy ending we didn't deserve.

In this study, we'll go from the prison of sin to the freedom and hope that is ours through the amazing grace of God. We never deserved God's goodness, and yet He extended it to us. All we had to do was receive it!

But by the grace of God I am what I am.

1 Corinthians 15:10 NKJV

CHAPTER ONE

THOU SHALT NOT!

"THE LAW IS HOLY, AND THE COMMANDMENT HOLY AND JUST AND GOOD."

Romans 7:12 NKJV

He's makin' a list, checkin' it twice. Gonna find out who's naughty and nice!" Sure, we all know this popular song that refers to Santa Claus. But how many of us have the very same view of God? We know God loves us and all, but we can't help but picture Him with a checklist on a clipboard. He's making His lists. Good deeds in one column, bad deeds in the other, like some kind of divine scorekeeper. When we're good, that counts in our favor. When we sin, there's a deduction from our score. Or perhaps we see Him as a referee, jogging along the sidelines of our life and watching our every move. If we put one toe over the line, He blows the whistle. Every time we step out of bounds, commit a foul, or break a rule, He jumps on it, bringing condemnation, shame, and guilt.

When we think about our heavenly Father in

CLEARING ↗ THE ↖ COBWEBS

Have you ever tried to do something that you wanted to come out absolutely perfect, but no matter how hard you tried, it was never quite right?

1

> *Because we live in a fallen world, we will experience negatives in our lives. Heartache and disappointment will come our way. We experience "stuff" we don't deserve, don't want, and can't send back. It's ours. But thanks be to God, nothing happens in this world that He doesn't know about and that He can't handle.*
>
> Thelma Wells

this way, our thinking is decidedly askew. It puts all the emphasis on our being good, on behaving ourselves, on winning God's approval. The Christian walk is not a matter of dos and don'ts, rules and regulations. Many people think that if the good we do in our lives outweighs the bad, then we've earned the right to enter heaven. But that's just not the case. Salvation isn't a matter of being good enough. It's a matter of God's goodness!

1. It's easy to see where all the emphasis on dos and don'ts comes from. After all, God started it! He gave commandments to His people and expected them to obey them. It was called "the Law."

- What was Joshua told to do with the Law in Joshua 1:8?

- What did Joshua tell the people to do with the Law in Joshua 22:5?

• What encouragement did Joshua offer in Joshua 23:6?

2. Paul assures us that the Law is a good thing. What does he say about it in Romans 7:12?

3. But while the Law is good, it does something surprising. What does Romans 4:15 tell us goes hand in hand with the Law?

> *If you want to describe grace in one word, it is Jesus. Grace (Jesus) is the answer for our guilt and failure. Grace (Jesus) is the strength we need to cope with life. Grace (Jesus) is the promise that gives us the hope that keeps us going.*
>
> Barbara Johnson

4. How does Romans 5:13 describe the unique relationship between the Law and sin?

5. How does Paul describe this interaction further in Romans 7:7–9?

*T*hose that focus on the finer points of the law put the discipline in spiritual discipline. Their teachings center on good moral behavior, clean living, and keeping all the commandments. But the best intentions in the world cannot boost us into sinless living. What's the point of setting up rules that no one can keep? To prove that we can't keep them. We're sinners, and we cannot save ourselves. One of the reasons the Law was given was to show us how far short we fall.

6. What's the point of all these "Thou shalt's" and "Thou shalt not's"? What did God tell His people in Leviticus 11:45?

7. And what did Jesus tell us in Matthew 5:48?

8. The standard is perfection, and it's beyond our reach. Do you find it a little discouraging that you can't keep the Law, even if you try? What did Paul admit in Romans 7:18?

9. If we *could* keep all the Law and live righteously on our own, what does Galatians 2:21 say becomes obsolete?

DIGGING DEEPER

God's standard is perfection, and there's no getting around that. But, praise the Lord, we're not the ones who have to *be* perfect. We're being *made* perfect!

- John 17:23
- Philippians 3:12
- 2 Corinthians 12:9
- Hebrews 10:14

Ponder & Pray

Nobody likes to have his shortcomings pointed out to him, but the Law forces us to face the facts. We're not perfect. We're not holy. We sin. Have you ever *thanked* God for His commandments? Have you ever thanked Him for all the Law? This week consider what your life might be like if there were no commandments—no Law. Would you admit to your sin? Would you try to live a good life in your own strength? Would you need God at all?

Trinkets to Treasure

At the close of each lesson, you will be presented with a small gift. Though imaginary, it will serve to remind you of the things you have learned. Think of it as a souvenir. Souvenirs are little trinkets we pick up on our journeys to remind us of where we have been. They keep us from forgetting the path we have traveled. Hide these little treasures in your heart, for as you ponder them, they will draw you closer to God.

Your trinket this week is a reverse reminder of today's lesson—a whistle. Though the Law of God demands perfection, points out our sin, and confirms our unworthy state, we need not be discouraged. God is not a referee on the sidelines, ready to blow the whistle on us whenever we fumble or fail. God is a God of patience, forgiveness, and grace.

NOTES & PRAYER REQUESTS

HEDGING

"WOE TO YOU, SCRIBES AND PHARISEES, HYPOCRITES! FOR YOU PAY TITHE OF MINT AND ANISE AND CUMMIN, AND HAVE NEGLECTED THE WEIGHTIER MATTERS OF THE LAW: JUSTICE AND MERCY AND FAITH."

Matthew 23:23 NKJV

ormal gardens are intriguing. Neatly laid out garden plots, beds of fragrant herbs, mossy statues, rose-covered bowers, trickling fountains, espaliered fruit trees, stone benches tucked into quiet corners. And hedges. Yards and yards of closely clipped hedges. Painstakingly pruned shrubs winding along the edges of each path. Low boxwood hedges around the herb garden. Pretty topiaries in geometric shapes. High privet hedges ensuring seclusion.

The Pharisees of ancient Israel were into hedging, but not the kind that needed constant clipping. They put up hedges around the Law of God. In order to prevent the breaking of one of God's commandments, traditions were established as a kind of buffer zone. For instance, if God's law forbade the coveting of another man's wife, then the men shrouded their women so that

CLEARING ⚐ THE ☙ COBWEBS

Have you ever been lost in a maze?

> *I certainly don't overtly resist the concept of grace, but I've tried to earn it a million times. I seem to cling tenaciously to the mistaken notion that I've got to be good enough in order to deserve grace.*
>
> Marilyn Meberg

no man could look on them at all. They reasoned that you couldn't lust after something you couldn't see. This was the hedge they set up around God's command. In this way, the Pharisees established a vast compendium of rules and regulations, and they prided themselves in knowing and keeping them all.

1. The Pharisees went nose to nose with Jesus on several occasions over the keeping of the Law. Inevitably, Jesus got the better of the hypocrites. What did He accuse them of in Mark 7:13?

2. What hypocrisy were the Pharisees guilty of in Matthew 23:23?

3. The Pharisees confronted Jesus, thinking they could put Him on the spot. What transgression did they accuse His disciples of in Matthew 15:2?

4. In the next verse, Jesus turns the tables by putting a pointed question to them. What does He ask in Matthew 15:3?

5. There was the Law—God's commandments found in Scripture—and then there were the traditions—a way of life handed down for generations. One pointed the way to righteous living. The other ensured the appearance of righteousness. Which did the Pharisees think was more important, according to Mark 7:8–9?

> *When we reach the end of our strength, wisdom, and personal resources, we enter into the beginning of His glorious provisions. And that's a wondrous place to be.*
>
> Patsy Clairmont

11

*L*et's say God charged you to tend a small garden for Him. You accept the task with pleasure and begin puttering among the fruit trees, rose bushes, and vines. But then, you worry over whether the garden is safe from foraging animals, so you plant a hedge around it and work diligently at keeping it clipped. But the hedge doesn't seem secure enough, so around that you build a fence. Then you have the brilliant idea of building a castle around the garden plot, making it a sheltered courtyard. Around the castle, a great wall is erected, with an iron gate to keep all away. Then you install a drawbridge and a moat, and ship in a bunch of crocodiles. You've made an impressive show of fulfilling God's charge. Meanwhile, the fruit drops rotting from the trees, the roses are cankered, and the weeds are choking out the vines. The whole time you were busy protecting your garden plot, you were neglecting it. Do you think this is what God intended?

> *Wherever you are now is God's provision, not His punishment. Celebrate this moment, and try very hard to do it with conscious gratitude.*
> Luci Swindoll

6. In Philippians 3:4–9, Paul lists all the earthly reasons he had to be confident in his own righteous living. What did he have to boast about?

7. What other tidbits about his former life does Paul tell us in Galatians 1:14?

8. Paul, as Saul the Pharisee, had it all together. He was a rising star on the religious scene. He had a promising career ahead of him. But what did he think of all of that, according to Philippians 3:7–8?

9. No amount of hedging can ensure a righteous life. What does 1 Peter 1:18–19 say does and does not redeem us?

> *The more I investigated God's love through the Scriptures the more I relaxed; the safety of His love untied the knot of anxiety and perfectionism within me.*
>
> Patsy Clairmont

13

DIGGING DEEPER

My junior high teacher was fond of the saying "I don't drink and I don't chew and I don't go with girls that do." He felt this quip was the epitome of pharisaical self-righteousness. Not one of us can ever be improved in God's eyes by what we do or don't do. In order to dig a little deeper today, read Galatians 3:10–24. What does Paul say in these verses about the law, justification, and Christ?

PONDER & PRAY

This would be a good time for some self-examination. Search your heart. Have you been trying to do the work that only grace can do? Have you been so busy protecting your image that you've neglected more important matters of the heart? It is the hidden person of the heart that God sees. No amount of hedging can change that.

TRINKETS TO TREASURE

Your trinket for this week could only be a pair of clippers—hedge clippers! It's too easy to live in a way that keeps up the appearance of a godly life. We know how to do and say all the right things. But God isn't impressed by our tidy hedges. He sees right into our hearts and knows what lies there. The Pharisees tried to bolster their own reputations and images but were denounced as hypocrites. We should not try to do what can only be done by God's grace!

NOTES & PRAYER REQUESTS

CHAPTER THREE

JUST DESSERTS

"THE WAGES OF SIN IS DEATH."

Romans 6:23 NKJV

he Wednesday night chil-
dren's program at our church
focuses on Scripture memoriza-
tion. The kids are assigned rather
lengthy passages from the Bible
and given incentives to study them
and commit them to memory. In my fifth-grade
class, the children earn chocolate bars if they're
able to say their week's verses. Quarterly, kids
who are able to say all their verses from memory
earn the chance to choose a prize from a treasure
chest full of toys. If at the end of the year they've
memorized every one of their passages, they earn
the ultimate reward—a trip to Six Flags with a
pocketful of spending money. Those children who
have dedicated themselves to memorizing their
verses get exactly what they deserve. They've
earned their prizes and fun. They're getting their
just desserts.

As sinners, we have nothing so pleasant to
look forward to. In fact, the only thing we are

CLEARING ⫷ THE ⫸ COBWEBS

It's amazing how
many things we think
we're entitled to in
life. What kinds of
things do you think
everyone deserves?

> *When a person comes to God,
> just as she is—while still in
> her sinning state—God looks
> at her and, because of what
> Jesus Christ did on the cross,
> he proclaims her righteous.
> She does not have to clean
> up her act. She does not have
> to do penance. All she has
> to do is believe God for the
> forgiveness of her sins.*
> Luci Swindoll

deserving of is death. Thankfully, as believers, we *don't* get our just desserts. God, in His goodness, extends grace to us, undeserving as we are.

1. There's no question that we're sinners. God can't pour out His grace and goodness in our lives until we recognize that fact and admit it.

• When does Numbers 5:6 say that we become guilty of sin?

• Are there degrees of bad—some sins being more acceptable than others? What does James 2:10 say?

• What does Isaiah 59:2 say our iniquities do?

2. When it comes to our sinful hearts, one thing leads to another. How does James 1:14–15 describe this process?

3. Sin has its inevitable end. What does Paul say sin earns us in Romans 6:23?

4. According to Scripture, sinners are worthy of death. Who, then, should we trust, according to 2 Corinthians 1:9?

> *It is a great treat in my day when I imagine that God is seeing me covered, smothered, and smoothed over with extravagant grace. All my rough edges are rounded in grace. All my imperfections are hidden by grace. All my frayed ends are tied up with grace. All that I'm lacking is filled up with grace.*
>
> Barbara Johnson

When I was little, my mother made me eat my vegetables. Or at least she tried. I had to at least taste those beets and squash and asparagus and peas. About the only thing that helped me choke them down was the knowledge that Mom had been baking that day. No veggies meant no dessert. Zucchini had slightly more appeal if I knew an apple pie was waiting. A clean plate meant I'd get my just desserts! As believers, Jesus traded places with us. He gives us a clean slate, and a clean slate means we'll get *His* just desserts.

5. According to Hebrews 2:9, what extraordinary provision did God make for the undeserving?

> When I am called to a behavior or attitude that is higher than my humanness, I'm comforted when I remember that it's not I, but He, who loves through me. Nevertheless, I need to get in concert with Him, and that means that my humanness must cooperate with His divineness.
>
> Marilyn Mseberg

6. What does 2 Timothy 1:10 say Jesus did to death?

7. What will happen to death, according to 1 Corinthians 15:54?

8. What picture do we get of our future in Revelation 21:4?

> God is offering Himself to you at a generous exchange rate: His forgiveness for your sins, His joy for your grief, His love for your loneliness. You will grow rich as you spend time with Him, listening for His voice.
>
> Barbara Johnson

9. What a change. We started this lesson acknowledging that we deserve to be separated from God forever. But because of God's goodness and grace, we need never be separated from Him again. Paul asks, "Who shall separate us from the love of Christ?" (Rom. 8:35 NKJV). What is the answer to his question, according to Romans 8:38–39?

DIGGING DEEPER

Though we shudder to look back at our graceless fate, we would do well not to forget the death sentence that once hung over our heads. When we remember what might have been, had Jesus not come to our rescue, we are all the more grateful for the grace in which we stand!

- Romans 7:5
- Romans 8:6
- 1 Corinthians 15:56

PONDER & PRAY

Mercy means not giving someone what he or she deserves. Grace is unmerited (unearned, undeserved) favor. This week, give all your thanks and praise to God for the evidence of mercy and grace in your own life. Consider all the ways in which the Lord has been good to you, and count each one of them as a blessing.

TRINKETS TO TREASURE

Those who want their just desserts learn how to clean their plates! And so our little treasure this week is a clean plate. This little doodad can help remind us that we should be grateful that we won't be receiving our just desserts. Jesus took our place and got what we had coming. He traded places with us, allowing us to receive His just desserts instead!

CHAPTER FOUR

AMAZING, BUT TRUE

"THROUGH HIM WE HAVE RECEIVED GRACE."

Romans 1:5 NKJV

ittle boys love dinosaurs. Sharp teeth, sharp horns, sharp claws. They're the ultimate monsters—real enough to be scary, but extinct enough to be safe. All the dinosaurs are reduced to fossils by now. Or have they? Have you heard the amazing but true fish story of the coelacanth (pronounced see-la-canth)?

Fishermen off the coast of South Africa were pulling in their nets one December day back in 1938, and pulled in something unexpected. It was big—more than five feet long—and ugly, and nobody on board knew what kind of fish it was. The captain, who was an enterprising fellow, thought this bizarre fish was unusual enough to bring it over to the lady who ran the local museum. She often paid good money for nice specimens. Ms. Latimer, the museum lady, couldn't find the strange fish in any of her books, so she wrote to one of the premier ichthyologists of the day,

CLEARING
⚲ THE ⚲
COBWEBS

Do you have a
favorite dinosaur?

> *Getting into heaven isn't*
> *dependent on our doing*
> *anything correctly, praise God!*
> *Redemption rests on the finished*
> *work of Christ on the cross.*
> Luci Swindoll

describing it. Dr. Smith recognized Ms. Latimer's description immediately, and the discovery rocked the scientific community. The coelacanth was thought to be extinct—gone the way of the dinosaur. But soon everyone had heard that the "dinosaur fish" was alive and well. Astonishing. Unforeseen. Unprecedented. Amazing. But true!

As sinners, we were doomed to extinction. Sentenced to death, worthy of wrath, separated from God. Nothing stood between us and the abyss. But then something unprecedented happened! Unforeseen mercy. Unmerited favor. Astonishing grace. And the sinner who had long been lost was found and given new life! Amazing, but true!

1. What's so amazing about grace? What does 2 Corinthians 8:9 have to say about it?

2. Jesus had all the riches of heaven, and yet He gave it up for us. What does Philippians 2:5–8 say that Jesus willingly did on our behalf?

3. What did Jesus do that the law could not, according to Acts 13:39?

4. Sin had reigned over us all, but all of that changed with Christ. What does Romans 5:20 say upset sin's dominance?

> *God has much greater ambitions for us than we have for ourselves. He laughs at our paltry plans, then plots to surprise us with the greatness of his grace.*
> Barbara Johnson

> *Once we realize what we've done, we begin to plead for mercy and forgiveness. Even though He's hurt and grieved about what we've done, He listens to our plea, wraps us in His loving embrace, and grants us unmerited favor—grace that is greater than all our sin.*
>
> Thelma Wells

5. And in Romans 5:21, this amazing turnaround is described in triumphant terms:

"As sin _____ in _____, even so might _____ through _____ to _____ _____ through Jesus Christ our Lord." (NKJV)

*I*t's the most famous, best-loved hymn of all time—"Amazing Grace." Its lyrics tell of the amazing transformation that grace works in our lives. "I once was lost, but now am found; Was blind, but now I see." Just when things were at their bleakest, everything was changed. A turning point was reached. In a moment, everything was new. By grace, we went from death row to divine adoption. From wretched to radiant. From unbelievable to undeniable. From lost to found.

6. Paul compares the actions of two different men in Romans 5:15. What were the consequences of their actions?

7. Grace is pivotal, foundational, essential to our faith. Paul knew grace's importance, and often opened and closed his letters with its mention. In this way, his epistles were bookended by grace. Here are a few openers. Paraphrase below what Paul is saying:

• Romans 1:7 –

• 1 Corinthians 1:3 –

• Galatians 1:3 –

• Philippians 1:2 –

• 1 Timothy 1:2 –

• 2 John 1:3 –

8. Grace becomes Paul's benediction as well. What does he pray at the close of these books?

• Romans 16:24 –

• 2 Corinthians 13:14 –

• Galatians 6:18 –

• Ephesians 6:24 –

9. *The Message* paraphrases the benediction of Galatians 6:18 to say, "May what our Master Jesus Christ gives freely be deeply and personally yours, my friends. Oh, yes!" God's grace is a very big idea to get our heads around. How can you make this theological truth deeply and personally yours?

DIGGING DEEPER

As one other song puts it, "There's no other word for grace but amazing." Amazing grace—one of the most familiar phrases in Christendom. We hear it all the time, but what does it mean to each of us individually? Take a few minutes to dig down in your own heart. What makes grace really amazing in your life? What turning point did grace bring in your heart?

PONDER & PRAY

In this day and age, it's pretty hard to impress people. Sometimes it feels as if we've seen it all. So when it comes to old, worn phrases like "amazing grace," we might actually wonder what there is to be amazed about. Pray this week for a renewed sense of awe and wonder over the changes that grace has wrought in your life. Ask the Lord to amaze you again!

TRINKETS TO TREASURE

Our trinket this week is a little toy dinosaur. He can remind us of the amazing comeback of the "dinosaur fish," the coelacanth, which once was lost but now is found. We, too, were faced with death and extinction, but we also discovered new life. There's no use denying it—grace really is amazing!

NOTES & PRAYER REQUESTS

CHAPTER FIVE

THE PRICE OF FREEDOM

"THE LAW WAS GIVEN THROUGH MOSES, BUT GRACE AND TRUTH CAME THROUGH JESUS CHRIST."

John 1:17 NKJV

Many of us are on a tight budget. We have so much to spend each month, and no more. And so we are careful with our money, stretching each penny so we can make it until the next paycheck. In the earliest days of our marriage, when I was new at planning meals and shopping for supplies, I walked through the grocery store with a calculator in my hand. I'd get the necessities first—bread, bananas, eggs, and carrots. Then stock up on household things—toilet paper, laundry soap, shampoo, and, later, diapers. Finally, I'd see how much was left over for little extravagances—strawberries, ice cream, or a watermelon. I had to count the cost of every item.

It's easy to count the cost of things that have stickers on them telling the price. But not everything comes with a clearly printed price tag. And

CLEARING ⁊ THE ⊱ COBWEBS

What items are you most tempted to buy off the impulse racks in grocery stores?

> *Christ became our bridge to God. Christ offers us daily assistance, divine opportunities, and eternal provision. He also extends to us his Word, which allows us to arch over this world's distorted mind-set to receive the pure wisdom that is from above.*
>
> Patsy Clairmont

not every cost is monetary. Grace is ours because of the goodness of God, but it came at a great cost—a price He paid for us.

1. God provided just one way for sins to be forgiven. What is that one way, according to Hebrews 9:22?

2. What was needed and is provided by our heavenly Father, according to Psalm 79:9 and Psalm 65:3?

3. Did God wait for us to clean up our act before sending Jesus to be the perfect sacrifice? What does Paul say in Romans 5:10?

4. What do we receive through the abundance of God's grace according to Romans 5:17?

5. Grace becomes all the more precious to us when we realize the cost that was paid so that it could be ours. What does Isaiah 53:12 say that Messiah would do?

*G*oing to college can be an expensive undertaking. Tuition, books, room and board—it all adds up quickly. But students in need can head to the financial aid office and apply for help. Sure, loans are available. But these must be paid off over time. Better still are scholarships. A scholarship is a gift. It covers the cost. It pays the debt. It pays one's way without expecting any payment in return.

Grace is not unlike a scholarship, for Jesus paid our way and made it possible for us to finish our course.

6. What did Jesus become for us, according to 2 Corinthians 5:21?

> *Thank heaven Christ came to rescue us from our smallness, our emptiness, our busyness, our loneliness, and our sinfulness.*
> Patsy Clairmont

7. How effective was Jesus' sacrifice according to Romans 6:10?

8. Jesus' triumph was complete! Through Him we enjoy all the riches of God's grace. What does Ephesians 1:7 say that includes?

9. According to Romans 5:2, Jesus has given us access into God's grace. This in itself is a reason for rejoicing, but what specifically does Paul say we can rejoice over?

DIGGING DEEPER

If there's one phrase I love in the book of Hebrews, it's "once for all." Jesus was able to take care of all our needs once and for all, and He only had to do it once. Once for all.

- Hebrews 7:27   • Hebrews 9:12
- Hebrews 10:10

Ponder & Pray

How long has it been since you counted the cost of your salvation? Spend time this week mulling over what Jesus gave up for you. Think about what He willingly endured for you. Ponder what He faced so that you wouldn't have to. Give yourself a chance to sit down and count and comprehend the price Christ paid for you.

✦ Trinkets to Treasure ✦

This week's trinket is a calculator. Whenever you see it, don't think of algebra or income taxes or tight budgets. Let it stand as a reminder to count the cost. Jesus paid a high price in order for us to be saved—the ultimate price. Yet He paid the cost willingly so that we could know God's grace.

CHAPTER SIX

FREE FOR ALL

"THANKS BE TO GOD FOR HIS INDESCRIBABLE GIFT!"

2 Corinthians 9:15 NKJV

When I was little, we used to make the long drive across state lines to visit my grandparents about once a year. We'd stay for a few days and visit all our favorite spots—the steps of the high school with its railings for sliding, the pier on the lakeshore with its lighthouse, and the water tower our uncle assured us was filled with root beer. Grandpa always took us to see the sights—the shop that sold frozen custard, the airstrip where small planes took off and landed, and Late's, which had the best hamburgers in town.

But best of all was Saturday morning, when Grandpa took us all to the new grocery store in town for breakfast. Why? Because on Saturday, this store pulled out all the stops and provided enough free samples to feed a family! There was a carnival-like atmosphere as we ranged up and down the aisles. Bags of doughnut holes, tiny sausages, slices of pizza, crackers with cheese,

CLEARING
↗ THE ↖
COBWEBS

What is one of the most memorable presents you ever received?

pickled herring, chicken cutlets, cookies, pretzels, fruit cocktail, spinach dip, sandwich spreads, and tiny ice cream cones. The store was always packed, and everyone who came was free to sample the food.

By God's grace, salvation is free to all who want it. But we get more than a sample. His grace abounds towards us, and we are given a new life— full and free.

> *God wants you to experience His grace whether you have faced your life with courage or with cowardice. Grace is not about us; it is about God. He will meet you wherever you are to help you take the next gutsy step.*
> Patsy Clairmont

1. To whom is grace available according to Titus 2:11?

2. There are a couple of key words that come into play when we're talking about grace. They show up in these verses:

Romans 3:24 – "Being justified _____ by His grace" (NKJV).

Ephesians 4:7 – "To each one of us grace was given according to the measure of Christ's _____" (NKJV).

3. What does Romans 5:18 say came to all men through Jesus' sacrifice?

4. Paul's description of grace in Ephesians 2:4–9 is one of the best and most concise. Fill in the blanks as you read through the verse and its parenthetical commentary.

God, who is _____ in mercy, (He has more than enough to cover our need)

because of His great _____ (no other can compare)

with which He _____ us, (each and every individual)

even when we were _____in trespasses, (uncaring, undeserving)

made us _____ together with Christ (made a way to life)

(by _____ you have been _____), (He came to our rescue)

and _____ us up _____, (risen like Jesus)

and made us _____ together (like friends and family)

in the _____ places in Christ Jesus, (where our real life is hidden)

that in the _____ to come (today and in the forever of eternity)

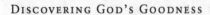

He might show the exceeding _____ of His _____
(greater wealth than the world can offer)

in His _____toward us in Christ Jesus. (He is so good to us)

For by _____ you have been saved (unmerited favor)

through _____, (when we believed)

and that not of _____; (we didn't earn it)

it is the _____of God, (it was all His idea)

not of _____, (not by righteous deeds)

lest anyone should _____. (as if we had something to do with it)

—Ephesians 2:4–9 NKJV

5. We've already looked at Romans 6:23, but let's take another peek at it. What does this verse say is the gift of God?

*I*t's the staple of many a mystery. The ransom note. When the bad guys make off with some wealthy woman's beloved Persian kitty cat, the ransom note is never far behind. It lists the demands of the kidnappers. Made from jumbled letters clipped out of the local newspaper and glued together: "If you ever want to see Fluffy again, put a hundred thousand dollars in unmarked bills in the dumpster behind Luigi's at midnight tonight." To set Fluffy free, all the demands must be met. If the exchange is made, Fluffy will be returned to her mistress.

Our lives were held ransom, and the demands were great. Still Jesus willingly paid the price for our freedom. Because of that, salvation is free for all who accept it.

6. What does 1 Timothy 2:6 say that Jesus did for us?

> *The wonderful thing about the Christian life is that we all enter freely. No matter who you are, where you're from, what your experience has been, Jesus Christ invites you to freely come. No conditions. No restrictions. No small print. No waiting. About this, you can be certain.*
> Luci Swindoll

7. Because of Jesus, salvation is free for all who come to Him. But not only that; those who come to Him are set free! What was prophesied in Isaiah 42:7?

8. And what is another messianic prophecy that Jesus came to fulfill, according to Isaiah 61:1?

9. Why does 2 Corinthians 5:15 say Jesus died for all of us?

DIGGING DEEPER

The price paid to set us free is inestimable, and yet salvation is free for the asking. We were slaves to sin, held captive by death, without hope. But Jesus' sacrifice opened up a door for us. Slaves were set free, death held no sting, and hopelessness became a thing of the past.

- Romans 6:18
- 1 Corinthians 6:20
- Romans 6:22
- 1 Corinthians 7:23

PONDER & PRAY

When you do a study on grace, you just find more and more reasons to be thankful for God's goodness and your salvation. This week, you can thank God that your freedom was free. There were no conditions, no strings attached, no hoops to go through, no requirements to meet. All we had to do was ask. It's all anyone has to do.

TRINKETS TO TREASURE

Our lives were held ransom by sin and death. We were captives, unable to pay the price freedom would cost. So our trinket this week is a ransom note. It will serve to remind us that though we were slaves, Jesus willingly paid the price for our freedom. Because of His sacrifice, our salvation is free.

NOTES & PRAYER REQUESTS

_____

_____

_____

_____

_____

_____

_____

_____

_____

_____

_____

_____

_____

_____

_____

_____

_____

_____

_____

_____

_____

CHAPTER SEVEN

CARTE BLANCHE?

"WHAT SHALL WE SAY THEN? SHALL WE CONTINUE IN SIN THAT GRACE MAY ABOUND?"

Romans 6:1 NKJV

arte Blanche. It's a French phrase that's been adopted into our English lexicon. I remember the fist time I ran across the phrase as a child reading *The Three Musketeers* by Alexander Dumas. The evil Milady had wheedled a *carte blanche* from Cardinal Richelieu, giving her permission to do away with the heroes of the story without any worry of repercussions. *Carte blanche* is defined as complete freedom or complete authority to act. A *carte blanche* gives someone unrestricted power to act at his or her own discretion. Milady's *carte blanche* would have let her get away with murder—literally!

Paul was concerned for new believers who thought that God's grace gave them a *carte blanche.* These men and women seemed to think that if God's forgiveness was so easy to come by, they could live in sin because they'd be covered by grace. They'd do as they pleased today, and

CLEARING ⊀ THE ⊱ COBWEBS

If someone gave you a blank check, what would you buy?

> *I worry sometimes that we as believers are more concerned with the appearance of righteousness than with the inner acquisition of righteousness. Celebrating the gift of grace means freeing oneself from the shackles of performance and luxuriating in the circumference of God's lavish acceptance.*
> Marilyn Meberg

apologize for it tomorrow. They reasoned, "The more I sin, the more opportunities there are for grace to flourish!" What began as a gift that was free for all quickly became a free-for-all!

1. What are we free from, according to Romans 8:2?

2. Now that we have been set free from the power of sin, we have amazing liberty. What does Paul say about our liberty in Galatians 5:1?

3. According to 2 Corinthians 3:17, those who have the Spirit of the Lord also have what?

4. So does liberty mean that we can do anything we like? What does Romans 6:1 have to say about that?

5. Paul is adamant that we understand this point, because he brings it up again in just a few verses. What does He ask in Romans 6:15?

> *I'm grateful Christ hasn't left us to flail about in our inadequacies, but instead He guides us toward transformation.*
>
> Patsy Clairmont

*D*uring the Middle Ages, the faithful would seek forgiveness from their sins by going to a priest. The man of God would hear their confession and help them to pray. But it didn't take long for greedy men to twist this tradition for their own gain.

People began selling indulgences. An indulgence supposedly guaranteed absolution from sins—for a small fee. Some people even purchased them in advance for sins they planned to commit later. The indulgence was the ultimate *carte blanche*.

> *One of the most touching scriptures is Galatians 4:6, in which God says to us, "Because you are sons, God sent the Spirit of his Son into our hearts, the Spirit who calls out 'Abba, Father.'" The Hebrew word abba means "daddy." We are reminded that we are never totally fatherless, and in times of quiet despair, we can cry out a prayer like this: "Daddy, oh, Daddy, comfort me, hold me. I so need Your touch. I so need Your tender presence. Be with me, dear Daddy. Let me rest in You, relax in You, and find peace in You."*
>
> Marilyn Meberg

6. We have liberty! By the grace of God we are free! But what does it mean to be free? Free to do what? What does Paul tell us our liberty should be used for in Galatians 5:13?

7. What does Peter warn in 1 Peter 2:16?

8. Paul offers an interesting way of looking at our "carte blanche" situation in Romans 6:18, 22. What does he say we have been set free to be?

9. Paul says that grace abounds in our lives to what end?

DIGGING DEEPER

We have been set free, but that doesn't mean we're at liberty to sin "that grace may abound." It can be tempting to take advantage of God's grace, rationalizing away our little indulgences, knowing that we can ask to be forgiven later. Take a little time now to compare and consider the message of two verses of Scripture—1 Corinthians 6:12 and Mark 4:19. What bearing do they have on this week's lesson and on your heart?

Ponder & Pray

There's an allure to complete freedom—doing whatever I want, whenever I want. The *carte blanche* and the indulgence are tempting offers. They invite us to set aside our better judgment, our responsibilities, our good sense, or even our standards, even for a little while. If we're honest with ourselves and honest with God, we know what's right and what's wrong. This week pray that God would help you understand what your life liberty should look like.

Trinkets to Treasure

Your gift this week is a blank check—a *carte blanche*. It reminds us that in Christ, we have liberty. But that liberty isn't a permission slip to pursue our own selfish interests. Grace was not given so that we could wreak havoc and let God clean up our messes for us. We do not sin so that grace can abound. Grace abounds toward us so that we can be free—free from sin, free to serve.

CHAPTER EIGHT

EXTRA CREDIT

"I DIDN'T WANT SOME PETTY, INFERIOR BRAND OF RIGHTEOUSNESS THAT COMES FROM KEEPING A LIST OF RULES WHEN I COULD GET THE ROBUST KIND THAT COMES FROM TRUSTING CHRIST—GOD'S RIGHTEOUSNESS."

Philippians 3:9 MSG

o you fly the friendly skies much? I never did before, but I've traveled a little more in the last two years, and I've made a startling discovery. Most people dread flying, and for very good reason. Long lines, long waits, long flights—they're almost more exhausting than the long drive would have been.

You clutch your boarding pass and shoulder your carry-on and file quietly onto the plane. The seats are narrow, and your knees touch the chair in front of you. Close quarters, stale air, and a crying baby two rows back. Your only consolation is a tiny glass of diet cola and a bag of pretzels. But on my last flight, I was bumped up to *first class*. Now, maybe you're the kind of gal who always flies first-class, but for those of you who don't, I thought you'd like to know what goes on up there! Sure, the seats were wider and there was decidedly more leg room, but the amenities didn't stop there. We were first to board and first to debark.

CLEARING THE COBWEBS

When's the last time you took an airplane flight? Where did you go?

There was a television screen that whirred down from somewhere in the ceiling, and it provided entertainment for we few, privileged travelers. My beverage—club soda with lime—came in a footed glass, and the stewardesses came around four times to refill it. While the passengers in coach were munching morosely on pretzels, I was served dinner on a tray. I had a cloth napkin, real silverware, and a fresh flower in a bud vase. I was being treated better than your average passenger.

Sometimes we think that there are various degrees of Christianity. Those who travel in coach are just your average Christians, but the truly dedicated, earnest believers get bumped up to first class. We want to be special, exceptional, better than average in God's eyes. And so we try to do what we can to earn a little extra credit. We hope to win God's favor by doing things to please Him. But the truth is, you can't impress God or make Him love you any more than He already does.

> *When we give ourselves to God—mind, body, soul, and spirit—He changes us. We cannot change ourselves. We don't have enough spiritual stamina to change ourselves, let alone another person or the world. But when the walls come down and He has access to the deepest parts of who we are, His love courses through us in a cleansing, holy way.*
>
> Nicole Johnson

1. Have you seen kids trying to impress their parents? "Look at me, Mom!" "Dad, watch me!" They vie for attention, admiration, accolades. They show off and boast, hoping to elevate themselves in their parents' eyes by their accomplishments.

- According to Romans 4:2, does God take our good deeds into account when it comes to salvation?

- What does Romans 3:27 say about our boasting?

- What is Paul's adamant stand on such boasting, according to Galatians 6:14?

> *We can take our eyes off ourselves and our own journey and realize that this is a group outing — that we are not supposed to arrive in heaven alone but hand in hand.*
>
> Sheila Walsh

2. Yet the temptation is there—to compare, to show off, to distinguish ourselves. And so we try to set ourselves apart from the crowd. In Bible times, this was done by obeying God's laws more thoroughly than anyone else. What were the Pharisees condemned for in Matthew 23:6–7?

3. What did the hypocrites do to impress their peers, according to Matthew 23:14?

> *God speaks to us clearly. He means what He says. What He says He'll provide, we can count on that. When He promises peace, wisdom, strength, or comfort, they are ours. God imparts His word and keeps it. His words matter! I find tremendous comfort in that.*
>
> Luci Swindoll

4. In their zeal to earn extra credit with God, what kind of nitpicking did the Pharisees practice, according to Matthew 23:23?

5. According to Matthew 23:25–26, what were the Pharisees trying to do, and what should they have done instead?

he Pharisees were definitely a group who loved to impress others. They liked to impress people at the Temple by lifting their eyes to heaven and praying in loud voices (Matt. 6:5). They dressed to impress, with their ornate tassels and dragging fringes (Matt. 23:5). And most of all, they tried to impress God. Paul knew what it was like to live that kind of life, but looking back he understood the foolishness of it. "I have been crucified with Christ. My ego is no longer central. It is no longer important that I appear righteous before you or have your good opinion, and I am no longer driven to impress God. Christ lives in me. The life you see me living is not 'mine,' but it is lived by faith in the Son of God" (Gal. 2:20 MSG).

> *We have to stand in the complexity of all that God is working on, not just in the simple part we can see for ourselves.*
>
> Nicole Johnson

6. Jesus gave us a parable about people who trusted in their own righteousness and thought they were better than those around them. What was the boast of the man in Luke 18:9–14? And what was Jesus' lesson to His listeners at the end of the story?

7. It's pretty obvious that we can never earn extra credit with God. What does Jesus urge us to do in Matthew 6:1?

8. How does Paul describe those who attempt to be justified by their deeds, according to Galatians 5:4?

9. What does Paul say about the grace of God in 1 Corinthians 15:10?

10. What does Paul say our boasting should be, according to 2 Corinthians 1:12?

DIGGING DEEPER

No extra credit. No bonus points. No upgrades. We can't improve our standing in God's sight. We don't have bragging rights, because we've got nothing to boast about!

- Romans 11:18
- Philippians 2:3
- Ephesians 2:9
- James 4:16

Ponder & Pray

As believers we're sometimes prone to "sibling rivalry" with our brothers and sisters in the Lord. Have you ever caught yourself comparing yourself to another believer? Have you ever had a momentary feeling of guilty gladness over someone else's struggles? This week, ponder the fact that we are all the same in God's eyes—beloved and precious. None of us can earn any more of His love. None of us can elevate ourselves by outstanding Christian behavior. Pray also for a clean vessel so that grace can transform you from the inside out.

Trinkets to Treasure

There's no such thing as a coach Christian and a first-class Christian. Our trinket this week is an airplane, to remind us not to try to elevate ourselves above those around us. Nothing we can do will ever make God love us any more than He already does. Conversely, nothing we can do will ever make God love us any less. We don't have to try to impress God. We can't earn any extra credit for good behavior.

CHAPTER NINE

No Strings Attached

"Now then, we are ambassadors for Christ."

2 Corinthians 5:20 NKJV

hen Pinocchio danced his way across the stage in his theatrical debut, he sang a catchy little tune. "I've got no strings to hold me down, to make me fret, or make me frown. I had strings, but now I'm free. There are no strings on me." Scripture presents grace to us as a free gift, no strings attached. But that's hard to understand. Nothing worthwhile is free, right? We've all been assured there's no such thing as a free lunch. The skeptic in us takes a look at God's free gift of grace and wants to know, "Where's the catch?" If we accept God's "free" gift, will we owe Him? Will He one day start asking for favors? Will we just become puppets, obliged to do whatever God asks of us? Does grace come with strings attached that will hold us down, make us fret, and make us frown?

CLEARING ⍅ THE ⍆ COBWEBS

Have you ever felt tied down by your responsibilities?

1. Are there times when God "calls in a favor" and compels us to do things for Him?

- What happened to Jesus in Mark 1:12?

- What was Paul compelled to do in Acts 18:5?

- According to 1 Corinthians 9:16, what does Paul say God compelled him to do?

> I encourage you as a fellow traveler to cherish and celebrate the gift of grace that calls you to draw near and to fall more in love with Jesus.
> Sheila Walsh

2. When we are compelled, we have the distinct impression that we must do or say something. Such things are not the strings attached to our salvation, but the working of God's Spirit in our hearts. What does Philippians 2:13 tell us about God's influence in our hearts?

3. When we become believers, we suddenly bear the name of Christ. We are called Christians. Paul urged the faithful to live up to the name we bear. What was his message to the church in Colossians 1:10?

4. This message was so important that Paul repeated it in several more of his letters.

Ephesians 4:1 – "I, therefore, the prisoner of the Lord, _____ you to _____ _____ of the _____ with which you were _____" (NKJV).

Philippians 1:27 – "Only let your _____ be _____ of the _____ of _____" (NKJV).

1 Thessalonians 2:12 – "That you would _____ _____ of God who _____ you into His own _____ and _____" (NKJV).

5. We're not puppets, tied to the strings that dictate our every move. When we talked about the freedom we have through grace, that was real. But when we make ourselves available to God, He can use us for His glory. Take a look at 2 Timothy 2:19–21.

- According to verse 19, who does the Lord know?

- In verse 20, what kinds of vessels are described?

• According to verse 21, if we turn from sin and make ourselves available to God, what can we become?

*S*peaking of strings, people are sometimes described as being tied to their mother's apron strings. This kind of attachment seems strange in a day and age when moms don't wear aprons anymore. But the gist of it isn't hard to grasp. When someone is tied to her mother's apron strings, she doesn't wander very far from her side. She lives to please her Mom, considering her opinion and her pleasure before making her choices. The phrase usually means that someone is still under the influence or domination of her mother. Though the world considers such an assessment as an insult, we can learn from it. For believers, it would be a good thing to remain tied to God's apron strings. Close by His side, under His influence, living to please Him.

6. What did Paul say he lived to do in Galatians 1:10?

7. What is our purpose according to 1 Thessalonians 2:4?

> *Each one of us needs a new beginning at some point or other. But it needn't come with a bang of fireworks or a streaking comet. New beginnings often come slowly.*
>
> Barbara Johnson

8. What does Hebrews 12:28 encourage us to do?

DIGGING DEEPER

We are a responsive people. When someone smiles at us, we smile in return. When someone shows us that he loves us, we look for ways to show him how much we care. Scripture says we love God because He loved us first. When we receive that love, we find ourselves looking for ways to show God how much His love means to us. And so we endeavor to please God.

- Romans 14:18
- 1 Thessalonians 4:1
- Hebrews 11:6
- 2 Thessalonians 1:11

PONDER & PRAY

Often we think of the strings that come attached to things as the things that tie us down. Sometimes our hearts rebel and long to be freed from such constraints. But there are ties that bind that are not at all bad. Love binds our hearts to that of another. The ties of friendship grow stronger over time. This week, ponder the ties that bind you to your Lord. Do you think of them as strings attached to salvation, or as the strengthening cords of a loving relationship? Be honest in telling God how you feel about such things. Ask Him to show you how to walk worthy of the name you bear. Pray, too, that you may be a vessel that God can use for His glory.

TRINKETS TO TREASURE

Those who are tied to their mother's apron strings are often called mama's boys. But as women who serve the Lord, we welcome the ties that bind us closer to our Father. We're not mama's boys, but Daddy's girls! To remind us of this, our trinket this week is an apron.

Notes & Prayer Requests

CHAPTER TEN

ONE OF THE FAMILY

"BEING HEIRS TOGETHER OF THE GRACE OF LIFE."

1 Peter 3:7 NKJV

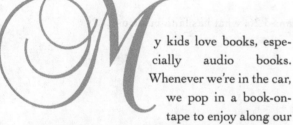

My kids love books, especially audio books. Whenever we're in the car, we pop in a book-on-tape to enjoy along our way. We've enjoyed silly stories and adventures, mysteries and classics, histories and horse stories.

One of their very favorite genres is what we like to call "orphan stories." These stories are terribly predictable, but that doesn't minimize our enjoyment of them. The orphan story always starts out the same way. A child of about ten years of age loses his or her parents. Suddenly, he or she must be shipped off to live with distant relatives. Sometimes it's an orphanage. Either way, the grieving orphan suddenly finds him- or herself at the mercy of someone who is cruel or uncaring. There's usually hunger, hard work, and hopelessness. Sometimes there's a friend—a streetwise ragamuffin who befriends and protects. Then there'll be a plot twist—a conspiracy to steal an inheritance, a twin separated at birth, a secret

CLEARING ⚹ THE ⚹ COBWEBS

Do you have a place where you always feel at home?

identity. But in the end, all is revealed. The wicked plot is uncovered. The police take away the bad guys. A kind, rich uncle comes to the rescue, or an estranged grandparent learns of the orphan's existence. The orphan and the ragamuffin are both adopted, so they can be both best friends and siblings forever. Any which way, the orphan is restored to a happy, loving home, and everyone lives happily ever after.

> *Grace finds us in our poverty and presents us with the gift of an inheritance we didn't deserve . . . the gift of grace.*
> Patsy Clairmont

Our lives aren't so different from that of the orphan. We were lost, helpless, hopeless. But in a supreme plot twist, we were rescued. A Father we didn't know we had saved our lives, gave us a new home, and adopted us to be His own children.

1. According to Galatians 3:26, what has faith made us?

2. By grace, we have more than just salvation. We have a sense of belonging. What characterizes a son of God, according to Romans 8:14?

3. According to 2 Corinthians 6:18, what does God say to those who believe?

4. Though Jesus is the only begotten Son of God, He made the way for what to happen, according to Ephesians 1:5?

5. Grace has worked an amazing transformation of our station in life! According to Galatians 4:4–7, what were we before, and what are we now?

> *We are the body of Christ, and deep inside each of us is a thirst to be known and loved, to be part of the stream of life.*
>
> Sheila Walsh

> *In every situation, whether*
> *ordinary or life threatening,*
> *God assures us that He keeps*
> *His eyes on us and knows the*
> *number of hairs on our heads.*
> *Absolutely everything that can*
> *happen to us—good, bad, or*
> *indifferent—God knows and*
> *cares about. God is concerned*
> *about us all the time, in every*
> *area of our lives, even if nobody*
> *else is. He promises that we are*
> *never away from His presence.*
>
> Thelma Wells

*Y*ou go to the mailbox one day, and there's a thick envelope from a very official--sounding law firm. There's a sheaf of papers inside, and the cover letter holds a bombshell. You have an uncle, a great-uncle, actually. He's been overseas for decades, which is why you'd never heard of him, but the long and the short of it is—you're his only heir. He recently passed away, and you've inherited every-thing. Land, titles, houses, jewels, and plenty of cash. Who wouldn't want to find out they have a long-lost uncle? To inherit amazing riches. Who wouldn't like to live a Cinderella story? To become royalty. Who wouldn't like to have a Daddy Warbucks? To be adopted by a loving father.

As believers, we've been adopted by our heavenly Father. We've been made daughters of the King. We, too, have an inheritance.

6. What kind of person would you choose to be your heir, if you had to choose someone? Who did God choose, according to James 2:5?

7. We are heirs. We've been adopted by God and have a part in His inheritance.

___ Acts 20:32   a. Through Jesus we have obtained an inheritance.

___ Romans 8:17   b. The Gentiles are fellow heirs through the gospel.

___ Galatians 3:29   c. By God's grace we have an inheritance.

___ Ephesians 1:11   d. Those who are called receive an eternal inheritance.

___ Ephesians 1:13–14   e. God qualified us to be partakers of the inheritance.

___ Ephesians 3:6   f. We are Christ's, and heirs according to the promise.

___ Ephesians 5:5   g. We are heirs of God and joint heirs with Christ.

___ Colossians 1:12   h. Sinners have no inheritance in the kingdom of God.

___ Hebrews 9:15   i. The Spirit is the guarantee of our inheritance.

8. "From the Lord you will receive the reward of the inheritance" (Col. 3:24 NKJV). Just what is this inheritance? What are we heirs to? What is Paul's hope in Ephesians 1:18?

9. Paul says we've "become heirs according to the hope of eternal life" (Titus 3:7 NKJV). How does Peter describe our inheritance in 1 Peter 1:4?

DIGGING DEEPER

By God's goodness and grace, we have become a part of His family. We're now heirs, and our inheritance awaits us in heaven.

- Matthew 6:19–20
- Luke 12:33–34
- Colossians 3:3
- Matthew 19:21
- 2 Corinthians 4:7

PONDER & PRAY

We tend to think of grace as a means of salvation. It's a theological term—definable, doctrinal, academic. But we sometimes forget just what grace has done for us personally. By God's grace we were saved, but by God's grace we were adopted. We're part of a family now—beloved children, rightful heirs. By grace we have a place we belong. Spend this week pondering this and thanking God for it!

TRINKETS TO TREASURE

We're one of the family now. We've been adopted, we're heirs, and we've got an eternal inheritance awaiting us. So this week, we'll make our trinket a nice, shiny jewel. It's not nearly as valuable or lasting as what we have in store, but think of it as a foreshadowing, a foretaste of greater glories.

NOTES & PRAYER REQUESTS

CHAPTER ELEVEN

FRIENDS OF GOD

"HE IS LORD OVER ALL LORDS, KING OVER ALL KINGS, AND THOSE WITH HIM WILL BE THE CALLED, CHOSEN, AND FAITHFUL."

Revelation 17:14 MSG

Family. You're born into one. You marry into one. You give birth to one. They're the people we're the closest to. We know them, and they know us. When it comes to parents, grandparents, in-laws, and children, we don't have a lot of choice in the matter. If you want to be nice about it, you could say God chooses our family for us; in His wisdom He places us where we belong. If you're more pessimistic, you could say we're stuck with our family. We can't get away from them. We are theirs, and they are ours—for better or for worse.

But what about friends? While families are birthed, friends are chosen. We have some say in who we want to get close to as a friend. Friends are the people we hang around with because we like them. Friends are the people we trust because they've earned our trust. Friends are the ones who know us best because we've let them see us for who we really are.

CLEARING ⊀ THE ⋇ COBWEBS

Who was your best friend when you were growing up?

We know we've become a part of God's family. He's our Heavenly Father, and we're His daughters. We know we belong. But isn't it even more precious to know that we can be friends of God? Not just born-again, not just adopted, but chosen as an individual to become a true friend of His.

1. Who was the first man in Scripture to be called a friend of God, according to James 2:23?

> *Dear friend, embrace your day—this day—it is a gift. Take the Lord's hand. He will help you to unwrap the day and then to celebrate it. And His grace will be sufficient for any need you have.*
>
> Patsy Clairmont

2. It's one thing to have history call you a friend of God. What is God's direct statement, recorded for us in Isaiah 41:8?

3. What was Moses able to do, a little later down the time line, according to Exodus 33:11?

4. God chose to get close to certain men. He walked in the Garden with Adam. He spoke directly to Noah. He considered Abraham to be His friend. Who did God choose in Acts 9:15?

5. Friends are chosen. We were chosen. How does 1 Peter 2:9 describe us?

*S*ome of us make friends more easily than others. For the outgoing gal, everyone's a friend. We can't step foot outside our house without stopping to chat with someone we know from somewhere along the way. For the quiet type, making friends takes time, and there are just a few who know us well enough to be called a friend.

Jesus knew the importance of having a circle of friends. He surrounded Himself with a dozen men throughout the years of His ministry. Of those twelve, three became even closer—Peter, James, and John are sometimes called Christ's inner circle. That's just another way of saying they were His best friends. We need friends too. Friendship matters.

6. What proverb, found in John 15:13, did Jesus fulfill?

7. What did Jesus consider to be a mark of our friendship with Him, according to John 15:14?

8. As we continue through this passage, what distinction did Jesus make in John 15:15?

9. According to Ephesians 1:6, what has God's grace done for us?

> *I pray that what I learn from the lives of others will be used by God to make me a more compassionate woman, more willing to serve, more grateful to God and of more use to others.*
>
> Sheila Walsh

DIGGING DEEPER

Being friends means being chosen. We are told from the time we are children to choose our friends carefully, because they have so much influence over us as we grow. We couldn't have a better friend than Jesus. But have you ever wondered why God would choose someone like us? His criteria for those He's chosen might be a bit different from ours.

- 1 Corinthians 1:27–28
- James 2:5

PONDER & PRAY

Friendships develop over time—time spent together. Things move from small talk and the weather to personal history and opinions to feelings and struggles as trust is built. What kind of friend are you to God? Do you give Him quick updates now and again—chitchat, breaking news, urgent needs? Or is He your close friend and confidant? As you ponder and pray your way through the week, consider just what it means to be a friend of God.

TRINKETS TO TREASURE

Every generation has seen its fads of the various tokens of childhood friendships. There've been friendship rings and friendship pins and friendship necklaces. Since the current fad runs to bracelets, let's make that our trinket this week. Your friendship bracelet can remind you just whose friend you are. Treasure your friendship, and spend the time needed to deepen and strengthen it.

CHAPTER TWELVE

EXTENDING GRACE

"LET US HAVE GRACE, BY WHICH WE MAY SERVE GOD."

Hebrews 12:28 NKJV

ave you ever had someone extend a small grace your way? A teacher hears your tale of woe and gives you an extension on your paper. Your paycheck peters out before the end of the month and your creditors extend a grace period. You're zipping down the on-ramp toward bumper-to-bumper rush-hour traffic on the freeway, and someone slows up so you can merge into the flow. The gal ahead of you in the checkout line sees that you only have a couple items and lets you go ahead of her and her overflowing grocery cart. A stranger sees you coming toward the door with arms laden with paraphernalia and he holds it open for you.

We can all be confident that God's grace abounds towards us. But like so many things in life, that grace doesn't have to stop there. In fact,

CLEARING THE COBWEBS

Which is harder for you—biting your tongue when you want to give someone a piece of your mind or speaking up when you could offer a few words of encouragement?

> *Are you pining for the fellowship that surpasses all others? Get yourself to the nearest Christian and connect. Spend time with other believers rejoicing over what you have in Jesus. Sing some songs. Laugh together. Pray for one another. Hug each other. Celebrate the blessed tie that binds you to one another in Christian love.*
>
> Marilyn Meberg

it's not meant to. Grace isn't just something we receive. It's something we can pass along. Paul says our lives are supposed to abound with grace. And that grace can be extended to others.

1. We usually think of grace as an intangible thing, but what did Barnabas see, according to Acts 11:23?

2. God extended His grace to us as a free gift. What does Matthew 10:8 encourage us to do?

3. In Hebrews 12:28, what does the writer say grace is able to do?

4. What does Romans 12:6 say that we have been given through grace?

5. What is Peter's admonition, found in 1 Peter 4:10?

> *That's the way life is, isn't it?*
> *We need each other. Scripture*
> *says two are better than one.*
> *We're instructed to love,*
> *pray for, care about, accept,*
> *forgive, serve, encourage,*
> *and build up one another.*
> Luci Swindoll

*W*hat does grace look like? In an everyday world, how can we spot grace in action? We are told that God produces fruit in our lives by His Spirit—tangible expressions of grace. Love, joy, peace, patience, kindness, goodness, faithfulness, gentleness, self-control. All of these things are extensions of God's grace. When our lives are characterized by such attitudes and we make a conscious decision to express these virtues into our dealings with others, we are extending grace.

6. Grace can be extended in very practical ways. What does Paul tell us to do in Colossians 4:6?

7. Our big mouths can get us into a lot of trouble at times. What further encouragement does Ephesians 4:29 give us?

8. Paul told young Timothy, "Be strong in the grace that is in Christ Jesus" (2 Tim. 2:1 NKJV).

- What does Paul want us to abound in, according to 2 Corinthians 8:7?

- How does God make this possible, according to 2 Corinthians 9:8?

9. What is Peter's prayer for all of us in 1 Peter 5:10? It can serve as a benediction for our study.

> *So often these days we hide within the walls of large churches. We come in as strangers and we leave the same way. We smile at one another, give the impression that we are the one family that has it all together, and go home to our private wars. Life is not meant to be that cold. We need each other badly.*
>
> Sheila Walsh

DIGGING DEEPER

Extending grace means giving something of yourself. Sometimes that means giving of your time or your attention or your energy. Giving often means using your gifts to help out a brother or sister in the Lord. Throughout the Scriptures, we are encouraged to give, and to give cheerfully!

- Mark 10:45
- Acts 20:35
- Luke 6:38
- 1 Timothy 6:18

PONDER & PRAY

Grace changed our lives in an amazing way, and it can continue to affect our daily dealings. As we wind down this study on receiving God's grace, take the time to look back over the lessons we've learned. Ponder the practical aspects of God's grace, and ask God to show you how you can extend it to those around you.

TRINKETS TO TREASURE

Extending grace means reaching out to those around us in the same way God reached out to us. That means showing mercy and kindness, even to those who may not deserve it. Our trinket this week is an open hand. We received grace freely from God's hand, and we are asked to extend it just as freely to those around us. Let this final treasure remind us that the grace we get is a grace we can give.

SHALL WE REVIEW?

Every chapter has added a new trinket to your treasure trove of memories. Let's remind ourselves of the lessons they hold for us!

1. A Whistle

God isn't a referee on the sidelines, ready to blow the whistle on us whenever we fumble and fail. Though the Law of God demands perfection, points out our sin, and confirms our unworthy state, we need not be discouraged. God is a God of grace.

2. Hedge Clippers

We know how to do and say all the right things—keeping up the appearance of a godly life. But God isn't impressed by our tidy hedges. He sees right into our hearts and knows what lies there. We should not try to do what can only be done by God's grace!

3. A Clean Plate

Those who want their just desserts learn how to clean their plates! We should be grateful that we won't be receiving our just desserts. Jesus took our place and got what we had coming. He traded places with us, allowing us to receive His just desserts instead!

4. A Dinosaur

This trinket can remind us of the amazing comeback of the "dinosaur fish," the coelacanth, who once was lost but now is found. We, too, were faced with death and extinction, but we also discovered new life. There's no use denying it—grace really is amazing!

5. A Calculator

This is a reminder to count the cost. Jesus paid a high price in order for us to be saved—the ultimate price. Yet He paid the cost willingly so that we could know God's grace.

 ## 6. A Ransom Note

Our lives were held ransom by sin and death. We were captives, unable to pay the price freedom would cost. The ransom note reminds us that though we were slaves, Jesus willingly paid the price for our freedom. Because of His sacrifice, our salvation is free.

 ## 7. A Blank Check

A *carte blanche* reminds us that in Christ, we don't have a permission slip to pursue our own selfish interests, but real liberty. We do not sin so that grace can abound. Grace abounds toward us so that we can be free—free from sin, free to serve.

 ## 8. An Airplane

There's no such thing as a coach Christian and a first-class Christian. Our trinket reminds us not to try to elevate ourselves above those around us. We don't have to try to impress God. We can't earn any extra credit for good behavior.

9. An Apron

Those who are tied to their mother's apron strings are often called mama's boys. But as women who serve the Lord, we welcome the ties that bind us closer to our Father. We're not mama's boys, but Daddy's girls!

10. A Jewel

We're one of the family now. We've been adopted, we're heirs, and we've got an eternal inheritance awaiting us. So for this week, our trinket was a nice, shiny jewel—a foretaste of greater glories.

11. A Friendship Bracelet

Your reminder of just whose friend you are. Treasure your friendship, and spend the time needed to deepen and strengthen it.

12. An Open Hand

Extending grace means reaching out to those around us in the same way God reached out to us. We received grace freely from God's hand, and we are asked to extend it just as freely to those around us.

Leader's Guide

Chapter 1

1. "This Book of the Law shall not depart from your mouth, but you shall meditate in it day and night, that you may observe to do according to all that is written in it" (Josh. 1:8 NKJV). Joshua is commanded to know the Law, to speak it, meditate on it, and do what it says. "Take careful heed to do the commandment and the law which Moses the servant of the Lord commanded you, to love the Lord your God, to walk in all His ways, to keep His commandments, to hold fast to Him, and to serve Him with all your heart and with all your soul" (Josh. 22:5 NKJV). Joshua later urges all God's people to do as he was instructed—know God's law; do what it says. But more than that, hang on to the God who gave the Law, giving Him all your heart. "Therefore be very courageous to keep and to do all that is written in the Book of the Law of Moses, lest you turn aside from it to the right hand or to the left" (Josh. 23:6 NKJV). Near the end of his life, Joshua's exhortations have changed little. Do what the Law commands! And here we find that Joshua says it takes courage to do so.

2. "Therefore the law is holy, and the commandment holy and just and good" (Rom. 7:12 NKJV). God's commands are as holy as He is holy. They are also just and good.

3. "Because the law brings about wrath; for where there is no law there is no transgression" (Rom. 4:15 NKJV). The Law, which we've established is a good and holy thing, brings about wrath! At first it might seem a little strange that something good can bring about something like the wrath of God. Don't worry, though, Paul continues to explain this in Romans.

4. "For until the law sin was in the world, but sin is not imputed when there is no law" (Rom. 5:13 NKJV). Aha! Now Paul's words are beginning to make sense. Put simply, sin was in the world, and people had been sinning since Adam and Eve fell. But before the Law was established, people couldn't be said to break that Law. You can't break the rules if there are none. So people merely did as they pleased.

5. "Well then, am I suggesting that the law of God is evil? Of course not! The law is not sinful, but it was the law that showed me my sin. I would never have known that coveting is wrong if the law had not said, 'Do not covet.' But sin took advantage of this law and aroused all kinds of forbidden desires within me! If there were no law, sin would not have that power. I felt fine when I did not understand what the law demanded. But when I learned the truth, I realized I had broken the law and was a sinner, doomed to die" (Rom. 7:7–9 NLT). Doesn't that sound just like kids? They automatically want to try whatever we tell them not to do! That's sin in our lives. When we know something is forbidden, we're drawn to it. The Law didn't create sin and it isn't sinful in itself. But it defined sin and pointed out the sin that was already in our hearts.

6. "For I am the Lord who brings you up out of the land of Egypt, to be your God. You shall therefore be holy, for I am holy" (Lev. 11:45 NKJV). God expected His people to be marked by holiness. Peter reemphasized this by quoting the Lord in 1 Peter 1:16—"It is written, 'Be holy, for I am holy'" (NKJV). Of course, they sinned too. That's why the system of sacrifices was set up in the tabernacle and later in the temple. Through those sacrifices, God's people were able to stand holy before a holy God.

7. "Therefore you shall be perfect, just as your Father in heaven is perfect" (Matt. 5:48 NKJV). The rules didn't change in New Testament times. God still demands holiness. But Jesus came with a promise that we could be perfect! As we will soon see, it was not our own perfection, but His perfect sacrifice that would satisfy God's requirement.

8. "For I know that in me (that is, in my flesh) nothing good dwells; for to will is present with me, but how to perform what is good I do not find" (Rom. 7:18 NKJV). If we become caught up in trying to keep all the rules, we're bound to become discouraged when we fail. Like Paul, we want to do what's right ("to will is present with me"), but we can't seem to keep it together.

9. "I do not set aside the grace of God; for if righteousness comes through the law, then Christ died in vain" (Gal. 2:21 NKJV). Think about it this way. When we try to live perfectly on our own—keeping all the rules by sheer willpower—we're snubbing God. It's as if we're saying, "Thanks, but I don't need grace, Lord! See? I can do this on my own!" God's Law, His commandments—they show us how far short we fall and humble us into acknowledging our unworthy state. If it were otherwise, then Jesus' sacrifice was useless, and He died in vain.

Chapter 2

1. Jesus accused the Pharisees of "making the word of God of no effect through your tradition which you have handed down" (Mark 7:13 NKJV). All the rules that the Pharisees had established over the years had thoroughly clouded people's understanding of God's own Law. You could say they distracted the people. All those traditions took up time and attention. It was hard work to meet men's standards. And while the people were wrapped up in meeting the manmade expectations, they never gave the actual Law of God a thought.

2. "Woe to you, scribes and Pharisees, hypocrites! For you pay tithe of mint and anise and cummin, and have neglected the weightier matters of the law: justice and mercy and faith" (Matt. 23:23 NKJV). I'm sure at the outset, these religious rulers had the best of intentions. They wanted to make sure the people didn't sin. But they focused too much on the details of obedience. They went so far as to tithe a tenth of the spices used in cooking their meals, but never looked beyond the minutia to see God's bigger plan.

3. "Why do Your disciples transgress the tradition of the elders? For they do not wash their hands when they eat bread" (Matt. 15:2 NKJV). Tradition demanded that the righteous go through a kind of ceremonial washing before a meal. The Pharisees, trying to pick out any failing in Jesus and His followers, actually confronted the Lord about His disciples' personal hygiene. God never said, "Thou shalt wash thy hands before every meal," let alone prescribed the proper manner in which to do so.

4. "He answered and said to them, 'Why do you also transgress the commandment of God because of your tradition?'" (Matt. 15:3 NKJV). Jesus didn't even dignify the quibbling Pharisees' question with an answer. Instead, He turned the question to them. Was God really concerned with the way someone washed his hands? No. But God was concerned with the cleanness of one's heart. Later, he called these outwardly fastidious Pharisees "white sepulchers"—clean enough on the outside, but filled with dead men's bones.

5. "'For laying aside the commandment of God, you hold the tradition of men—the washing of pitchers and cups, and many other such things you do.' He said to them, 'All too well you reject the commandment of God, that you may keep your tradition'" (Mark 7:8–9 NKJV). The Pharisees had traded the righteousness of God for the admiration of men. They preferred to appear good in the eyes of other men. Tradition was more important to them than God.

6. "If anyone else thinks he may have confidence in the flesh, I more so: circumcised the eighth day, of the stock of Israel, of the tribe of Benjamin, a Hebrew of the Hebrews; concerning the law, a Pharisee; concerning zeal, persecuting the church; concerning the righteousness which is in the law, blameless" (Phil. 3:4–6 NKJV). Paul had had the best of everything. The best background, the best neighborhood, the best school, the best position. He'd jumped through all the right hoops. He'd made all the right connections. He'd never known failure. He was considered a righteous man, blameless before God.

7. "I advanced in Judaism beyond many of my contemporaries in my own nation, being more exceedingly zealous for the traditions of my fathers" (Gal. 1:14 NKJV). Paul, as Saul then, had risen through the ranks. He was climbing the social ladder. He was a mover and a shaker. He had distinguished himself and was destined for greatness.

8. "But what things were gain to me, these I have counted loss for Christ. Yet indeed I also count all things loss for the excellence of the knowledge of Christ Jesus my Lord, for whom I have suffered the loss of all things, and count them as rubbish, that I may gain Christ" (Phil. 3:7–8 NKJV). Paul gave it all up. He walked away from his promising career. He waved aside the opinions of his comrades. All his former ambitions seemed pointless now. Paul had come face-to-face with Jesus, and all the former glories were rubbish in comparison. Paul chose Jesus.

9. "Knowing that you were not redeemed with corruptible things, like silver or gold, from your aimless conduct received by tradition from your fathers, but with the precious blood of Christ, as of a lamb without blemish and without spot" (1 Peter 1:18–19 NKJV). Here is the crux of the matter. We can't depend on earthly things to save us. We can't buy redemption with money. We can't live in a way that makes us worthy of being saved. Redemption comes only through the blood of Christ. His sacrifice makes our salvation possible. Everything else is rubbish.

Chapter 3

1. "When a man or woman commits any sin that men commit in unfaithfulness against the Lord, and that person is guilty" (Num. 5:6 NKJV). In this passage, sin is equated with unfaithfulness to God. Any sin that can be committed is an act of unfaithfulness that makes us guilty. "For whoever shall keep the whole law, and yet stumble in one point, he is guilty of all" (James 2:10 NKJV). Even if you are mostly good, but sin in some small matter, you're just as guilty as the worst of criminals. There are no big sins and little sins. Sin is sin. "Your iniquities have separated you from your God; and your sins have hidden His face from you, so that He will not hear" (Isa. 59:2 NKJV). Sin separates us from God.

2. "But each one is tempted when he is drawn away by his own desires and enticed. Then, when desire has conceived, it gives birth to sin; and sin, when it is full-grown, brings forth death" (James 1:14–15 NKJV). In the *New Living Translation*, these verses read, "Temptation comes from the lure of our own evil desires. These evil desires lead to evil actions, and evil actions lead to death." James explores the inner workings of our hearts. Our sinful desires tempt us, and so we sin. And sin brings death.

3. "The wages of sin is death" (Rom. 6:23 NKJV). Those who sin are deserving of death. The Message puts an interesting slant on this verse. "Work hard for sin your whole life and your pension is death."

4. "Yes, we had the sentence of death in ourselves, that we should not trust in ourselves but in God who raises the dead" (2 Cor. 1:9 NKJV). Who better to trust when one is dying than One who can raise the dead. Here we get our first hint of hope!

5. "We see Jesus, who was made a little lower than the angels, for the suffering of death crowned with glory and honor, that He, by the grace of God, might taste death for everyone" (Heb. 2:9 NKJV). This verse beautifully tells the story of grace. Jesus, who is God, was made a man. He suffered and died on our behalf. He tasted death for all people.

6. "Our Savior Jesus Christ, who has abolished death and brought life and immortality to light through the gospel" (2 Tim. 1:10 NKJV). Jesus didn't just die. He wasn't just raised from the dead. Jesus abolished death! Where there was only death in our future, we now see life and immortality stretching out into eternity.

7. "So when this corruptible has put on incorruption, and this mortal has put on immortality, then shall be brought to pass the saying that is written: 'Death is swallowed up in victory'" (1 Cor. 15:54 NKJV). Death will be no more. Jesus triumphed over it, and it will be swallowed up in victory.

8. "God will wipe away every tear from their eyes; there shall be no more death, nor sorrow, nor crying. There shall be no more pain, for the former things have passed away" (Rev. 21:4 NKJV). No more death. We who were deserving of death will never feel the threat of it again. Death will be abolished. Swallowed up in victory. And we will live with Jesus forever! What an amazing grace!

9. "I am persuaded that neither death nor life, nor angels nor principalities nor powers, nor things present nor things to come, nor height nor depth, nor any other created thing, shall be able to separate us from the

love of God which is in Christ Jesus our Lord" (Rom. 8:38–39 NKJV). Nothing. Nothing will ever separate us from God again.

Chapter 4

1. "For you know the grace of our Lord Jesus Christ, that though He was rich, yet for your sakes He became poor, that you through His poverty might become rich" (2 Cor. 8:9 NKJV). Trading places. Jesus gave up His riches and became poor so that those sunk in poverty might become rich. I call that amazing.

2. "Christ Jesus, who, being in the form of God, did not consider it robbery to be equal with God, but made Himself of no reputation, taking the form of a bondservant, and coming in the likeness of men. And being found in appearance as a man, He humbled Himself and became obedient to the point of death, even the death of the cross" (Phil. 2:5–8 NKJV). Jesus gave it all up—His place at God's side, His home in heaven, His reputation. And instead, He became a man. Then He became a sacrifice. He died horribly so that we wouldn't have to. He did this all on our behalf.

3. "And by Him everyone who believes is justified from all things from which you could not be justified by the law of Moses" (Acts 13:39 NKJV). We couldn't keep the law, and so the law did not justify us before God. But Jesus justifies us, for His sacrifice fulfilled the requirements of the law.

4. "Moreover the law entered that the offense might abound. But where sin abounded, grace abounded much more" (Rom. 5:20 NKJV). What a good before-and-after verse! Where sin had reigned, grace triumphed.

5. "As sin **reigned** in **death**, even so **grace** might **reign** through **righteousness** to **eternal life** through Jesus Christ our Lord" (Rom. 5:21 NKJV).

6. "For if by the one man's offense many died, much more the grace of God and the gift by the grace of the one Man, Jesus Christ, abounded to many" (Rom. 5:15 NKJV). In this passage, Paul compares Adam and Jesus. By Adam's sin, one man brought sin and death to all men. By Jesus' sacrifice, one Man brought grace and life to all who would receive it.

7. "Grace to you and peace from God our Father and the Lord Jesus Christ" (Rom. 1:7 NKJV). "May God our Father and the Lord Jesus Christ give you his grace and peace" (1 Cor. 1:3 NLT). "So I greet you with the great words, grace and peace" (Gal. 1:3 MSG). "We greet you with the grace and peace that comes from God our Father and our Master, Jesus Christ" (Phil. 1:2 MSG). "Grace, mercy, and peace from God our Father and Jesus Christ our Lord" (1 Tim. 1:2 NKJV). "Grace, mercy, and peace will be with you from God the Father and from the Lord Jesus Christ, the Son of the Father, in truth and love" (2 John 1:3 NKJV).

8. "The grace of our Lord Jesus Christ be with you all" (Rom. 16:24 NKJV). "The grace of the Lord Jesus Christ, and the love of God, and the communion of the Holy Spirit be with you all. Amen" (2 Cor. 13:14 NKJV). "Brethren, the grace of our Lord Jesus Christ be with your spirit. Amen" (Gal. 6:18 NKJV). "Grace be with all those who love our Lord Jesus Christ in sincerity. Amen" (Eph. 6:24 NKJV).

9. We can talk about God's grand scheme and the foundational importance of grace to Christianity, but we need to also think about how grace affects us each individually, personally. Is "grace" a bit of Christian jargon that's too hard to define or explain? Or is grace a familiar mercy that you cannot imagine living without? What has this amazing grace accomplished in your life?

Chapter 5

1. "According to the law almost all things are purified with blood, and without shedding of blood there is no remission" (Heb. 9:22 NKJV). For sin to be forgiven, blood had to be shed. The wages of sin was death, and a death was required. That is why a system of sacrifices had been established for the people of God in Old Testament times. The shed blood of animals was needed to atone for the sins of the people.

2. "Help us, O God of our salvation, for the glory of Your name; and deliver us, and provide atonement for our sins, for Your name's sake" (Ps. 79:9 NKJV). Atonement was needed. In another psalm, it says, "As for our transgressions, You will provide atonement for them" (Ps. 65:3 NKJV).

God provided a way for the people to receive atonement for their sins. He made a way for them to be forgiven.

3. "For if when we were enemies we were reconciled to God through the death of His Son, much more, having been reconciled, we shall be saved by His life" (Rom. 5:10 NKJV). We were enemies of God when Jesus died—not friends or even acquaintances.

4. "For if by the one man's offense death reigned through the one, much more those who receive abundance of grace and of the gift of righteousness will reign in life through the One, Jesus Christ" (Rom. 5:17 NKJV). Righteousness that was not our own.

5. "He poured out His soul unto death, and He was numbered with the transgressors, and He bore the sin of many, and made intercession for the transgressors" (Isa. 53:12 NKJV). Jesus paid the price for all our sins. He'd never sinned all His life, but He was heaped with sin, wrath, and death in our places.

6. "For He made Him who knew no sin to be sin for us, that we might become the righteousness of God in Him" (2 Cor. 5:21 NKJV). Jesus, who had never sinned in all His life, took on all the sins of the world. Paul says He became sin for us so that we might become righteous before God.

7. "For the death that He died, He died to sin once for all; but the life that He lives, He lives to God" (Rom. 6:10 NKJV). Once for all. Jesus took care of sin once and for all. No further sacrifice is needed. Grace triumphed in one fell swoop!

8. "In Him we have redemption through His blood, the forgiveness of sins, according to the riches of His grace" (Eph. 1:7 NKJV). Through grace we have redemption. Through grace, we are forgiven. And through grace, we shall have life!

9. "Through whom also we have access by faith into this grace in which we stand, and rejoice in hope of the glory of God" (Rom. 5:2 NKJV). We can rejoice in hope of the glory of God. Put simply, we can rejoice because we have hope of eternal life. We shall live forever. We shall see God in all His glory. We shall live with Him. Sinners whose wages were nothing but death now hang on to the promise of eternal life with God.

Chapter 6

1. "The grace of God that brings salvation has appeared to all men" (Titus 2:11 NKJV). Grace is available to all who want to receive it.

2. "Being justified **freely** by His grace" (Rom. 3:24 NKJV). "To each one of us grace was given according to the measure of Christ's **gift**" (Eph. 4:7 NKJV). Say them together: free gift! Grace is free to all who will receive it. And grace is a gift we didn't expect or deserve.

3. "Therefore, as through one man's offense judgment came to all men, resulting in condemnation, even so through one Man's righteous act the free gift came to all men, resulting in justification of life" (Rom. 5:18 NKJV). Here we see it again: free gift. Jesus' sacrifice brought grace, and this free gift brought justification and life.

4. "God, who is **rich** in mercy, because of His great **love** with which He **loved** us, even when we were **dead** in trespasses, made us **alive** together with Christ (by **grace** you have been **saved**), and **raised** us up **together**, and made us **sit** together in the **heavenly** places in Christ Jesus, that in the **ages** to come He might show the exceeding **riches** of His **grace** in His **kindness** toward us in Christ Jesus. For by **grace** you have been saved through **faith**, and that not of **yourselves**; it is the **gift** of God, not of **works**, lest anyone should **boast**" (Eph. 2:4–9 NKJV).

5. "For the wages of sin is death, but the gift of God is eternal life in Christ Jesus our Lord" (Rom. 6:23 NKJV). We often focus on the first half of that verse, "the wages of sin" part. But the second half of Romans 6:23 holds an incredible promise. God's gift to us offsets sin's price. God gives us the gift of life—eternal life!

6. "Who gave Himself a ransom for all" (1 Tim. 2:6 NKJV). He paid the price. He took our place. He set us free.

7. "You will open the eyes of the blind and free the captives from prison. You will release those who sit in dark dungeons" (Isa. 42:7 NLT). We were the people waiting in darkness. Sin was like a prison, and we were in with a death sentence. Jesus came to release us from the dark dungeon in which we were imprisoned.

8. "The Spirit of the Lord God is upon Me, because the Lord has anointed Me to preach good tidings to the poor; He has sent Me to heal the brokenhearted, to proclaim liberty to the captives, and the opening of the prison to those who are bound" (Isa. 61:1 NKJV). Jesus confirmed that He fulfilled this prophecy in Luke 4:18.

9. "He died for all, that those who live should live no longer for themselves, but for Him who died for them and rose again" (2 Cor. 5:15 NKJV). Jesus sacrificed His life for our sake. He died so that we could live. In this verse, Paul gives us a glimpse of what the Lord wants us to live for. Not for ourselves, but for Him. The new life that has opened up before us is one that brings Him glory.

Chapter 7

1. "For the law of the Spirit of life in Christ Jesus has made me free from the law of sin and death" (Rom. 8:2 NKJV). We've covered this already and it's pretty clear. We're free from sin and death.

2. "Stand fast therefore in the liberty by which Christ has made us free, and do not be entangled again with a yoke of bondage" (Gal. 5:1 NKJV). It's so easy to go back to the old way of doing things. The Lord doesn't want us to live as slaves after He's set us free. When we receive His grace, old things are passed away. We can hold on to that promise.

3. "Now the Lord is the Spirit; and where the Spirit of the Lord is, there is liberty" (2 Cor. 3:17 NKJV). Another verse to confirm that freedom is ours when we belong to the Lord.

4. "Well then, should we keep on sinning so that God can show us more and more kindness and forgiveness?" (Rom. 6:1 NLT). In the next verse, Paul's answer to this question is emphatic—"Of course not!" (NLT), "I should hope not!" (MSG), "Certainly not!" (NKJV), "God forbid!" (KJV), "No!" (NCV).

5. "What then? Shall we sin because we are not under law but under grace? Certainly not!" (Rom. 6:15 NKJV). Some in the early church were twisting the gospel of grace and using it to rationalize away their sinful ways. Some even asked forgiveness in advance for the sins they planned to commit later. We cannot live in sin knowing that we can be forgiven for it later. That's not the kind of freedom grace is meant to bring.

6. "For you, brethren, have been called to liberty; only do not use liberty as an opportunity for the flesh, but through love serve one another" (Gal. 5:13 NKJV). Ah! We're not set free to run amok. We're set free for a purpose! God (who loved us enough to send His Son to die so that we could have grace and freedom and life) set us free so that we can love and serve. We live for Him now, and our changed lives bring glory to His name.

7. "As free, yet not using liberty as a cloak for vice" (1 Peter 2:16 NKJV). Peter backs up Paul here. We shouldn't use our Christian liberty as an excuse to cater to our own little vices.

8. "And having been set free from sin, you became slaves of righteousness" (Rom. 6:18 NKJV). "Now having been set free from sin, and having become slaves of God, you have your fruit to holiness, and the end, everlasting life" (Rom. 6:22 NKJV). Does it bother you to think of yourself as a slave? It doesn't have to. We are free to serve a new Master. Where there was only death before, now there is fruitfulness and eternal life.

9. "God is able to make all grace abound toward you, that you, always having all sufficiency in all things, may have an abundance for every good work" (2 Cor. 9:8 NKJV). God's grace abounds in our lives. It provides all we need for what we are called to do. God, in His infinite grace, has given us the oomph we need to do what He has called us to do. We are called to do good for His glory, and He gives us the grace we need to do it.

Chapter 8

1. "Was it because of his good deeds that God accepted him? If so, he would have had something to boast about. But from God's point of view Abraham had no basis at all for pride" (Rom. 4:2 NLT). Abraham didn't earn God's blessings any more than we can. We're not saved on our own merits, so we have nothing to boast about. "Can we boast, then, that we have done anything to be accepted by God? No, because our acquittal is not based on our good deeds. It is based on our faith" (Rom. 3:27 NLT). Faith negates our ability to boast. As Paul says in Ephesians 2:9, "not of works lest anyone should boast" (NKJV). "But God forbid that I should boast except in the cross of our Lord Jesus Christ, by whom the world has been crucified to me, and I to the world" (Gal. 6:14 NKJV). You want to boast? Then boast about Jesus. Pile all the glory on Him, for He's the only one who deserves it!

2. "They love the best places at feasts, the best seats in the synagogues, greetings in the marketplaces, and to be called by men, 'Rabbi, Rabbi'" (Matt. 23:6–7 NKJV). What a bunch of show-offs. They go out to mingle, to see and be seen. They love to be honored. They delight in VIP seating. They enjoy the respectful nods of those they pass by. They enjoy their elevated status in the community.

3. "Woe to you, scribes and Pharisees, hypocrites! For you devour widows' houses, and for a pretense make long prayers. Therefore you will receive greater condemnation" (Matt. 23:14 NKJV). For all their eloquence, the hypocrites were praying to the room, not to the Lord. I can't read this verse without thinking, Busted! The Lord, who knew their prayers, also knew how empty they were.

4. "Woe to you, scribes and Pharisees, hypocrites! For you pay tithe of mint and anise and cummin, and have neglected the weightier matters of the law: justice and mercy and faith" (Matt. 23:23 NKJV). In their eagerness to perform every aspect of the laws and traditions, the Pharisees actually tithed at the table. Before seasoning their food, they'd count each grain of salt, each leaf of mint, each granule of every herb and spice, reserving a tenth for the Lord. They were obsessive about such miniscule concerns, yet ignored the more important things, like justice, mercy, and faith.

5. "Woe to you, scribes and Pharisees, hypocrites! For you cleanse the outside of the cup and dish, but inside they are full of extortion and self-indulgence. Blind Pharisee, first cleanse the inside of the cup and dish, that the outside of them may be clean also" (Matt. 23:25–26 NKJV). The Pharisees were all about appearances. Everything they did was intended to improve their image and impress the masses. But Jesus branded them as hypocrites. What good is a pretty cup if the inside is filthy? God is more concerned with the hidden parts. When the inside of the vessel is clean, then the rest will follow.

6. The Pharisee went to the temple to thank God for making him better than others and to give Him a list of his latest accomplishments. "God, I thank You that I am not like other men—extortioners, unjust, adulterers, or even as this tax collector. I fast twice a week; I give tithes of all that I possess" (Luke 18:11–12 NKJV). I like the way his manner of prayer is worded here: "The Pharisee stood and prayed thus with himself." Really, he seems to be carrying on a monologue of self-congratulation instead of a prayer. The Pharisee is compared to the humble tax collector, who trembled to come near to God, kept his eyes downcast, and beat his breast as he pleaded for forgiveness. Jesus ends His object lesson by telling His listeners that only one of these two men was heard, forgiven, and justified.

7. "Take heed that you do not do your charitable deeds before men, to be seen by them. Otherwise you have no reward from your Father in heaven" (Matt. 6:1 NKJV). On the one hand, we have a warning here. God doesn't reward us if we do the right thing for the wrong reasons. However, there is a promise here too. Our Father in heaven sees us when we do things for Him, and He will reward us for them in His time.

8. "You have become estranged from Christ, you who attempt to be justified by law; you have fallen from grace" (Gal. 5:4 NKJV). Paul says that these people have fallen from grace.

9. "But by the grace of God I am what I am, and His grace toward me was not in vain; but I labored more abundantly than they all, yet not I, but the grace of God which was with me" (1 Cor. 15:10 NKJV). As believers, we

are new creations, and we are what we are because of God's grace. Even the good things we do are possible by God's grace working in our lives. It's all because of grace.

10. "For our boasting is this: the testimony of our conscience that we conducted ourselves in the world in simplicity and godly sincerity, not with fleshly wisdom but by the grace of God, and more abundantly toward you" (2 Cor. 1:12 NKJV). Even if we boast that we've obeyed God and lived sincerely, we cannot forget that it is by the grace of God. Grace is the foundation of everyone's testimony.

Chapter 9

1. Sometimes the Bible uses the word compelled or constrained when it comes to doing things for God. "The Holy Spirit compelled Jesus to go into the wilderness" (Mark 1:12 NLT). "Paul was compelled by the Spirit, and testified to the Jews that Jesus is the Christ" (Acts 18:5 NKJV). "For preaching the Good News is not something I can boast about. I am compelled by God to do it. How terrible for me if I didn't do it!" (1 Cor. 9:16 NLT). Wow! Here are men who were sensitive to God's desires. They felt the prompting, the urgency, the compulsion to do God's will. Did they *have* to do it? No. We all have a choice. But did they want to do God's bidding? Yes.

2. "For it is God who works in you both to will and to do for His good pleasure" (Phil. 2:13 NKJV). We still have a choice. We'll always have to choose. There's a difference between putting conditions on our salvation (we are assured salvation is a free gift) and the work of God's salvation in our hearts. The things we find ourselves wanting to do for God are the natural consequences of a grateful heart and a growing relationship.

3. "That you may walk worthy of the Lord, fully pleasing Him, being fruitful in every good work and increasing in the knowledge of God" (Col. 1:10 NKJV). Walk worthy. Live worthy. Live in such a way that you don't dishonor the One whose name you bear. The way we live reflects on the One we claim to live for!

4. "I, therefore, the prisoner of the Lord, **beseech** you to **walk worthy** of the **calling** with which you were **called**" (Eph. 4:1 NKJV). "Only let your **conduct** be **worthy** of the **gospel** of **Christ**" (Phil. 1:27 NKJV). "That you would **walk worthy** of God who **calls** you into His own **kingdom** and **glory**" (1 Thess. 2:12 NKJV).

5. "Nevertheless the solid foundation of God stands, having this seal: 'The Lord knows those who are His,' and, 'Let everyone who names the name of Christ depart from iniquity.' But in a great house there are not only vessels of gold and silver, but also of wood and clay, some for honor and some for dishonor. Therefore if anyone cleanses himself from the latter, he will be a vessel for honor, sanctified and useful for the Master, prepared for every good work" (2 Tim. 2:19–21 NKJV). There are all kinds of people in the body of believers, and we each have a place in God's house. Some of us have more prominent positions, and some of us serve in what seems to be a humble role. But these verses say that when we turn from sin and set ourselves apart to serve God, we become useful to Him. He is able to do good and bring glory to Himself through our lives.

6. "Obviously, I'm not trying to be a people pleaser! No, I am trying to please God. If I were still trying to please people, I would not be Christ's servant" (Gal. 1:10 NLT). Paul lived to please God. The opinions of others weren't important to him. He kept his eyes on God's good pleasure.

7. "Our purpose is to please God, not people. He is the one who examines the motives of our hearts" (1 Thess. 2:4 NLT). We exist to please God and bring glory to His name. At times, that may sound rather generic—as if we're disposable lackeys who follow mindlessly. But remember! God made us each uniquely, loves us each completely, and prepared a way for us to be with Him forever. As in any relationship, there is both give and take going on. Don't balk at what seem to be strings. Grace is still grace, and it is a free gift.

8. "Since we are receiving a Kingdom that cannot be destroyed, let us be thankful and please God by worshiping him with holy fear and awe" (Heb. 12:28 NLT). Just look at all that is ours by God's grace! How do we respond to these precious promises? By living with grateful hearts.

By worshiping God. And by living to please Him. These are not strings attached to our salvation. They are the natural outpouring of a heart that responds to the heavenly Father.

Chapter 10

1. "For you are all sons of God through faith in Christ Jesus" (Gal. 3:26 NKJV). By His grace, we are sons and daughters of God.

2. "For as many as are led by the Spirit of God, these are sons of God" (Rom. 8:14 NKJV). When we were saved, we received God's Spirit. He is with us and leads us, and is a sign of our position as sons and daughters of God.

3. "I will be a Father to you, and you shall be My sons and daughters, says the Lord Almighty" (2 Cor. 6:18 NKJV). What precious words!

4. "Having predestined us to adoption as sons by Jesus Christ to Himself, according to the good pleasure of His will" (Eph. 1:5 NKJV). Jesus made a way for us to be adopted. We're now a part of His family—brothers, sisters, joint heirs.

5. "But when the fullness of the time had come, God sent forth His Son, born of a woman, born under the law, to redeem those who were under the law, that we might receive the adoption of sons. And because you are sons, God has sent forth the Spirit of His Son into your hearts, crying out, 'Abba, Father!' Therefore you are no longer a slave but a son, and if a son, then an heir of God through Christ" (Gal. 4:4–7 NKJV).

6. "Has God not chosen the poor of this world to be rich in faith and heirs of the kingdom which He promised to those who love Him?" (James 2:5 NKJV). God is fond of doing the unexpected. Or perhaps it's just that we don't think like He does. But God chose the poor to be heirs to all His wealth. He chose those who needed it the most.

7. c, g, f, a, i, b, h, e, d

8. This verse is a part of one of Paul's prayers, filled with the things he wants believers in all the churches to understand. He often begins these prayers with the phrase, "May you understand…" And one of the things he wants us to understand is "what are the riches of the glory of His inheritance in the saints." We've inherited great riches, a glorious inheritance. We know a part of this glorious inheritance is the eternal life we have been promised. But beyond that, our wildest imaginations couldn't dream up what God has in store!

9. "An inheritance incorruptible and undefiled and that does not fade away, reserved in heaven for you" (1 Peter 1:4 NKJV). We may not know exactly what is in store, but we can know that our inheritance is pure, eternal, unbreakable, and awaiting us safe in heaven. By grace we were saved, adopted, and made heirs. Because of God's grace, the treasures of heaven await us.

Chapter 11

1. "'Abraham believed God, and it was accounted to him for righteousness.' And he was called the friend of God" (James 2:23 NKJV). What an epitaph! Abraham is remembered and respected for many things, but to be called the friend of God—what a privilege.

2. "But you, Israel, are My servant, Jacob whom I have chosen, the descendants of Abraham My friend" (Isa. 41:8 NKJV). God calls Abraham His friend.

3. "So the Lord spoke to Moses face to face, as a man speaks to his friend" (Ex. 33:11 NKJV). Moses conversed with God while leading his people to the promised Land. He spoke to God face-to-face, as a friend.

4. "He is a chosen vessel of Mine to bear My name before Gentiles, kings, and the children of Israel" (Acts 9:15 NKJV). Paul. He saw Jesus. He was caught up to heaven in visions. He penned much of our New Testament Scriptures. Why? Because God chose him.

5. "You are a chosen generation, a royal priesthood, a holy nation, His own special people, that you may proclaim the praises of Him who called you out of darkness into His marvelous light" (1 Peter 2:9 NKJV). Chosen. Royal. Set apart. Special. Called. We are different from the rest of the world because of Him whose friend we are.

6. "Greater love has no one than this, than to lay down one's life for his friends" (John 15:13 NKJV). Jesus died for us before we even knew Him, but because He did, we can be His friends.

7. "You are My friends if you do whatever I command you" (John 15:14 NKJV). Friends are trustworthy, dependable, true. And friends, over time, begin to emulate one another. Jesus didn't want any fair-weather friends. Those who were truly friends of His would be recognizable to the world because they'd follow His lead. Live as He'd want them to live. Emulate Him. Obey Him.

8. "No longer do I call you servants, for a servant does not know what his master is doing; but I have called you friends, for all things that I heard from My Father I have made known to you" (John 15:15 NKJV). We're not following Jesus blindly. He's given us all we need to know. Do you realize that our Bibles reveal to us all we need to know? Do you realize that we know how the story will end? Christ showed us His heart, told us His plans, made us His confidants. Jesus made us His friends.

9. "To the praise of the glory of His grace, by which He has made us accepted in the Beloved" (Eph. 1:6 NKJV). We are among God's beloved. He holds us close and considers us His friends. All this is possible because of grace.

Chapter 12

1. "When he came and had seen the grace of God..." (Acts 11:23 NKJV). What did Barnabas see? Grace. Or more accurately, the evidence of grace in the lives of believers.

2. "Freely you have received, freely give" (Matt. 10:8 NKJV). Grace has been extended to us. We received it freely. Now we are called to extend grace to others.

3. "Let us have grace, by which we may serve God acceptably with reverence and godly fear" (Heb. 12:28 NKJV). By grace, we can serve God. That's something we can see and do. Grace works in our hearts, but it reaches out through us to those who need our love and care.

4. "Having then gifts differing according to the grace that is given to us, let us use them" (Rom. 12:6 NKJV). We've been equipped by grace to reach out to others. We've received gifts to use as we serve God.

5. "As each one has received a gift, minister it to one another, as good stewards of the manifold grace of God" (1 Peter 4:10 NKJV). We aren't given these gifts so that we can set them on our mantels or lock them in our display cases. God's gifts are always practical—meant to be put to good use. Paul's admonition is sensible. Use your gifts!

6. "Let your speech always be with grace, seasoned with salt, that you may know how you ought to answer each one" (Col. 4:6 NKJV). What could be more practical than extending grace whenever we speak? Let your speech be with grace. Think before you speak. Choose words filled with grace.

7. "Let no corrupt word proceed out of your mouth, but what is good for necessary edification, that it may impart grace to the hearers" (Eph. 4:29 NKJV). Here we have it again. Our words need to be consciously chosen with grace in mind. We need to speak encouragement.

8. "But as you abound in everything—in faith, in speech, in knowledge, in all diligence, and in your love for us—see that you abound in this grace also" (2 Cor. 8:7 NKJV). Paul's prayer for us is that we would abound in grace. "And God is able to make all grace abound toward you, that you, always having all sufficiency in all things, may have an abundance for every good work" (2 Cor 9:8 NKJV). We can't muster up our own grace. We can only extend the grace God gives. He makes grace abound to us!

9. "May the God of all grace, who called us to His eternal glory by Christ Jesus, after you have suffered a while, perfect, establish, strengthen, and settle you" (1 Peter 5:10 NKJV). God is the God of all grace. He gives us grace and makes grace abound in our lives. What's more, through that grace, God is able to do good work in our lives. He perfects us, establishes us, strengthens us, and settles us. All of this happens while we await the ultimate promise of grace—eternal glory with Him.